I LOVE TAMAGOTCHI

The Unofficial Guide to the world's smartest electronic pets

BRONWEN KOMATSUBARA
Illustrated by Paul Davies

World International Limited

All rights reserved. No part of this publication may be reproduced or transmitted by any means, electronic, mechanical, photocopying or otherwise, without the prior permission of the publisher.

Created exclusively for World International Limited by Broadcast Books. First published in Great Britain in 1997 by World International Limited, Deanway Technology Centre, Wilmslow Road, Handforth, Cheshire SK9 3FB.

Copyright © Text Bronwen Komatsubara
Copyright © Illustrations Paul Davies

The moral rights of the author and illustrator have been asserted.

A CIP catalogue record for this book is available from the British Library.

ISBN 0-7498-34781
10 9 8 7 6 5 4 3 2 1

Cover and text design by AB3
Printed and bound in Great Britain by
Biddles Ltd, Guildford and King's Lynn

The publishers acknowledge that Kabushiki Kaisha Bandai has made an application for the trade mark Tamagotchi.

CONTENTS

I LOVE MY TAMAGOTCHI

You know, I wasn't expecting to be any good with virtual pets, but I got one for my birthday and we got on really well. I called him Migi, and we had many happy times together. A lot of my friends had tamagotchi and digipets as well, but none of theirs lasted as long as Migi, so people started coming to me for advice.

I never went to a special egglet school or anything like that, so in the beginning the advice I gave people was really just common sense. I still say the most important thing in rearing a tamagotchi is that you have to love it, because if you're in love, it's impossible to do anything wrong. Just treat your egglet the way you'd like to be treated, and you'll be fine.

But as people got more and more involved with their egglet, they started to ask harder questions. *Could they exercise their virtual pet? Were too many Snacks bad for it? What should they do if their egglet misbehaved? How long do virtual pets live for?* And so on.

My house became a sort of egglet farm, where I could

rear virtual pets and look after lost tamagotchi while we waited for their owners to come and collect them. And eventually I wrote this book, so that people who lived far away from me would benefit from my experiences, and learn from my mistakes before they made errors of their own.

The only real problem was my brother Ken, who can be very annoying and is extremely cruel to virtual pets. But even that can be an advantage, because if you find out what my brother Ken does wrong, you won't do it yourself.

So if you're really serious about virtual pets, you've come to the right place. I hope you enjoy my book and find it useful. Please remember that everything in this book is only my opinion, and is not *guaranteed* to improve your life with your egglet. These are some of the methods and tactics that have worked for me, and if they work for you too then that's great. But don't take everything I say to heart like it's the Ultimate Truth; this isn't a bona fide Official Guide. Every virtual pet is different, and the only person who really, truly knows how to deal with it is the pet's original owner. I hope that some of my suggestions prove helpful, and that you enjoy reading this book as much as I have enjoyed writing it.

So if you want to know more about those lovely little creatures called eggypets, virtual pets, digipets, gigipets, egglets (my favourite word) or (the original and best) tamagotchi, just keep on reading!

THE STORY OF VIRTUAL PETS

You're probably wondering exactly how egglets came into the world. Well, it's quite a long story, and it's been told so many times that it's become a little bit garbled. Anyway, this is how it happened, as told to me by my dad. I think he might have embellished it in a few places to stop me falling asleep, but if you read this you'll get the general idea.

Once Upon a Time ...

Once upon a time, there was a big company called Bandai that made toys for children. One of the best jobs you could wish for was sitting around thinking of new toys that the company could make. Every day could be just like Christmas. It was hard work, but a lot of fun, and the people who came up with the best ideas became very famous. One of those people was a lovely lady called Aki Maita.

Aki thought it would be a nice idea to combine pets and toys, and started thinking about all the different kinds of things that people were buying.

Electronic gadgetry is all over the place these days, with mobile phones, personal stereos and radio pagers. We also have electronic toys like screensavers, computer games, including the pocket-sized Gameboy made by Bandai's rival Nintendo. Then there are the simulation games where you have to run a city, or a planet, or a hospital. We get a lot of these from abroad, but there was a very famous one in Japan when I was tiny called Princess Maker where the idea of the game was to bring up a child to be a nice person. And on the Gameboy there's this thing called Pocket Monster where you have to raise a, well, a monster.

Aki tried to think of something that would really appeal to the people who buy these devices and games, but also something that would be fun. The answer was supplied by a very Japanese concern.

Space. We don't have very much of it. The middle of Japan is one great big national park. Hundred and hundreds and hundreds of square miles of forests and lakes and mountains. Unfortunately, the mountains kind of win out and you can't actually build any houses there because it's too steep. So instead, most Japanese people live on The Flat Bit, which is a thin line of ground running around the coast. There are two Big Flat Bits, called Tokyo and Osaka, but that's about it. So we've got 120 million people, all crammed into a tiny area.

This means we don't have much room for parks and playgrounds. In fact, some schools have put their playgrounds on the roof to save space. It also means we don't have much space for pets. Despite the fact that everybody loves a cute little pet to keep them company, it's rather difficult for the Japanese, because if we had a big enough house, we wouldn't have a park to take the pet for walks, and if we had a park, we wouldn't have enough time to do it because we all work so hard.

So Aki thought it would be a neat idea if she could make an electronic pet. It would be like having a radio pager, but if it bleeped at you it wouldn't be a message from someone you knew, it would be your electronic pet looking for attention. You wouldn't need to take it for walks in a non-existent park, you could sneak it into school with you because it would fit in your pocket, and it would even be a pet that you could play with on a crowded train.

The people at Bandai liked the sound of Aki's idea, and sent her off to try it out. Aki and her friends spent two years thinking and arguing about it before they came up with an idea that everybody liked. After that, it took another year to program it so that there were no nasty mistakes or strange goings-on in the circuitry. The biggest problem for Aki was sorting out the box it came in. After all, no one had ever made an electronic pet before so she had no idea how it ought to look. Aki and her friends went down to a big shopping district in Tokyo called Shibuya and jumped out at passing schoolgirls to ask them what they thought. After trying out thirty different designs, they decided that the egg-shaped casing was the nicest, which is why they came up with the name 'tamagotchi', which means 'lovable egg' or 'egg watch'.

By the way, if you have more than one of them, they're still called 'tamagotchi'. There's no need to put an 's' at the end in Japanese, so it's a bit like 'sheep'. No one says 'sheeps', and no one says 'tamagotchis' either.

An Egglet is Born!

After three long years, the tamagotchi were ready for the world, and Aki proudly took the first one to show to the rest of the company. Some people weren't very impressed. They thought it was ugly, they thought it was a waste of time, and they didn't think that children would find it very interesting. But enough of them trusted Aki to put the tamagotchi on sale.

That was on the 20 November 1996. Aki was very pleased with her tamagotchi, but even she had no idea how popular it would be. People were going crazy over tamagotchi, and not just the Shibuya schoolgirls that Aki was aiming for. Boys, girls, businessmen and career women, they all went mad over the chance to own an electronic pet of their own. Reports came back to Bandai that there weren't enough egglets to go around, and 5,000 people a day called to ask where they could buy them.

I was one of the lucky ones who managed to get one of those precious early egglets. I followed the instructions, hatched it and immediately fell in love with it for ever. And, because I'm a hard-working person, I did my very best to treat my tamagotchi as well as possible. People used to come round to my house to see it. They offered me lots of money for it, but I refused to part with my beloved egglet.

Everyone was very envious of me, and resolved to get a tamagotchi of their own. The moment a shop announced it was going to receive a shipment, the queues would start to form outside. The shops were selling out of egglets before they could even put them on the shelves. People started to pay silly money for tamagotchi. There were reports of people paying ten times the normal price just to get their hands on one.

Virtual Cats and Dogs

And then the copycats started. Someone rang me and said: 'Hooray, I've got a virtual pet of my own now, and me and my dog are very happy together.' Now I was in a pretty bad mood anyway because my brother

Ken never, ever answers the phone and I had been rather busy washing my hair at the time. But when I heard that, I knew something was very wrong. 'What do you mean, you and your dog?' I said. 'They don't make dog tamagotchi!'

'Yes they do,' said the caller. 'I know they do, because I've got one. And my friend's got a cat ...'

'A cat!?'

'Yeah, and *his* friend's got a kind of alien thingy.'

'Listen,' I shouted, putting all thoughts of hair mousse behind me. 'They do not do dogs, they do not do cats, and they do not do alien thingies. If you've got any of those then you've got a ... fake.'

My voice sunk as I reached the end of the sentence, because I realized there might be a lot of trouble on the horizon. I told my dad immediately, and he just laughed and told me I was over-reacting. As you can probably guess from my name, I'm only half Japanese, so sometimes I don't act in a typically Japanese way. Sometimes it gets me into trouble at school, like when someone thinks the red bits in my hair are dyed when they're actually natural. And in the case of the imitation tamagotchi, I hadn't thought about honour and duty and stuff like that.

Dad laughed and said that I was just like my mother when I lost my temper for no reason. He explained that in Japan, excellence was a matter of honour. You couldn't stop anyone from making something *like* a tamagotchi, but tamagotchi were unique and special and took time to get right. They also grew into loads of different creatures every time, not a single useless dog or a ratty old cat. Tamagotchi would always be best, and if people bought something inferior they would eventually see the error of their ways.

International Egglet

By this time, the fame of tamagotchi was spreading far and wide, and people all over the world were desperate to own one. The original egglets were still selling like hot cakes, but there still weren't enough to go round and a lot of people were still buying the copycat versions. There was a time when in some countries, especially in the Far East, there were more copycats than real tamagotchi. But there were now five factories around the world, working around the clock to make more , so more and more people in my town were getting tamagotchi of their own. And for some reason, whenever they had a problem with their electronic pets, they would come and ask my advice. I even became a bit of a local celebrity!

One day, I was coming home from school when I saw my friend Rei playing with a strange egglet design. It looked like one the originals, not a copycat, but it wasn't a colour that I had seen before.

'What's that scarlet thing?' I asked her.

'It's not scarlet,' said Rei sniffily. 'It's rhodamine red, with, I might add, yellow buttons.'

We both went to a very expensive school which stuffed our brains full of all sorts of clever things every day, but even I had to look 'rhodamine' up for myself in the dictionary. But that wasn't the point. The point was that there were lots of tamagotchi types in Japan by this time. There were yellow ones with orange buttons, see-through green ones with blue buttons, see-through blue ones with yellow buttons, blue and yellow clock-face ones (with numbers on the front), pink and blue clock-face ones, light orange ones, light blue ones and even the highly prized all-white one with black buttons. But there was no such thing as a rhodamine red one with yellow buttons. Not in Japan anyway.

'And just where exactly,' I continued, 'did you find this rhodamine red tamagotchi?'

'Oh,' said Rei proudly, because she'd been waiting all day for someone to ask, 'my dad went to America on business and he brought this back for me.'

I took a look at the tamagotchi, and, sure enough, saw that all the writing on it was in English, and not in Japanese. Luckily for Rei, I was able to translate for her and tell her that her American egglet was hungry.

The moment I got home, I ran up to Dad and put on my poshest Japanese.

'Honourable Father,' I wheedled. 'Your humble and worthless daughter was just wondering what's going on with these American tamagotchi. I await your wise counsel, so tell me, I beseech you.'

'Stop talking funny, Bronwen,' muttered Dad. 'I read about them in the paper this morning. They're special export-version tamagotchi Bandai are selling in foreign countries. They've been selling them in America and Europe, but would you believe it! A lot of them are getting sold to Japanese people who are bringing them back here!'

Luckily for everyone, there were eventually seven factories around the world churning out tamagotchi for the eager public. And finally there were enough tamagotchi to go round in Japan, and people in foreign countries could have their own and not worry about Japanese businessmen buying them up and shipping them home for their children.

Bandai got to work making new breeds of egglet, and I could finally get on with the arduous task of making my hair look lovely and shiny.

But it didn't stop there. Because the love of tamagotchi brought people together in friendship and harmony, which is the kind of thing that Japanese people just flip their lids about. And I kind of half flip my lid about it, for genetic reasons, you understand.

And my dad was right, of course. Because people eventually gave up on the copycat tamagotchi and bought the genuine article, as it was simply the first and the best. And we all lived happily ever after.

Egglet Expert

Except that more and more people were asking for my advice. And now that tamagotchi were abroad, relatives from the other side of my clan started ringing up in the middle of the night. And while it was kind of nice to hear from all those far-flung bits of my mother's family that never bother to call normally, I started to worry again. My foreign relatives called me for advice because I was a fully-fledged egglet expert (more by luck than judgment), and what's more, a member of the family. But what  about all those people who didn't know me? How would they get their questions answered?

And that'll be you. Hello. My name is Bronwen Komatsubara and it's very nice to meet you. Let's talk about virtual pets. Pay attention, because there will be a quiz later.

THE SCREEN

Your virtual pet lives inside the screen of the egg-shaped casing. Surrounding the screen are eight different icons that you can access to keep your pet fit and well, check up on it and see how it's feeling.

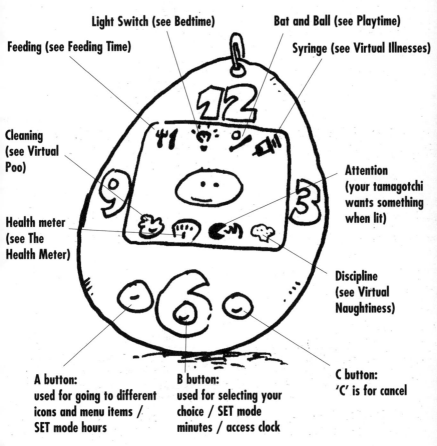

Light Switch (see Bedtime)

Bat and Ball (see Playtime)

Feeding (see Feeding Time)

Syringe (see Virtual Illnesses)

Cleaning (see Virtual Poo)

Attention (your tamagotchi wants something when lit)

Health meter (see The Health Meter)

Discipline (see Virtual Naughtiness)

A button: used for going to different icons and menu items / SET mode hours

B button: used for selecting your choice / SET mode minutes / access clock

C button: 'C' is for cancel

For more information on life with your virtual pet, just keep reading ...

HATCHING

When you first receive your egglet, it should be carefully packaged in plastic to keep it safe. The instructions might look daunting at first, but it's a good idea to make sure you know what you're doing before you pull out the paper tab that starts it going. Nobody wants their pet's first experience of planet Earth to be one of hunger and loneliness, but that's exactly what it'll be unless you already know how to take care of it.

The paper tab keeps the batteries from running low before there's anyone around to look after the tamagotchi properly. Once you pull the tab out, you should see a throbbing egg sitting on the screen. This is your tamagotchi getting ready to hatch, and it might take up to five minutes before it actually plucks up the courage to come out into the world. Don't panic, this is quite natural, and young tamagotchi are likely to be a little scared about the experience.

Occasionally, you may find that nothing happens when you pull out the tab. This means that your egglet has fallen asleep inside the egg, and that it's been inside for so long that it might need a little coaxing. In such cases, the best thing to do is to turn the casing round and reset it. On the back you will see a little hole, and you will need to gently nudge it with a pointy object like the end of a pen or one of the spines on a fork. On our tamagotchi farm, we use a Japanese chopstick, which, unlike the Chinese variety, has a slightly pointy end that fits snugly into the hole. Don't jab too hard, you don't want to hurt the poor little thing after all, but do give it a gentle poke to remind it that it's supposed to be starting on the glorious journey that is a tamagotchi's life.

Some egglet owners can get a bit fidgety waiting for their pet to pop out, but there are some vital tasks you can get on with while you're waiting for the tamagotchi to arrive. The most important is to make sure that the clock is set properly. Your egglet should be very happy living inside the screen, but the only way it can tell what time it is in the world outside is by looking at the clock. Press the B button to call up the clock, then press the A and C buttons at the same time to get into the SET mode. When the word SET appears on the screen, you're ready. Use the A button to pick the right hour, and the B button to pick the right minute. Don't get too carried away clicking the buttons round to the right time. It's all too easy to accidentally go one number too far, and then you'll have to go all the way around again. Also, make sure that you don't get AM and PM mixed up. If, for example, it's three in the afternoon but your clock reads AM, your tamagotchi will actually think it's three o'clock in the morning, and this will make it very confused.

The first time my brother Ken ever hatched a virtual pet, he rushed straight in and lived to regret it. Instead of reading the instructions, he snatched the egglet out of the package, ripped out the paper tab and started pressing all the buttons. He watched the egg for a couple of minutes, then got bored and went away in a huff. His tamagotchi popped out when it was good and ready, and luckily I was there to welcome it with a few treats and games. When Ken came back in, he snatched it back and played around with it himself, but he didn't tell me that he hadn't set the clock. Ken got a nasty surprise in the middle of the night, because his poor egglet thought it was lunch-time and wanted some food. Needless to say, Ken wasn't very happy about it, and neither was I, because he hadn't read the instructions and that meant yours truly had to get up and show him how to feed it.

THE HEALTH METER

There are several ways you can tell how your egglet is feeling. If you've just won a game with it, or cleared away a particularly nasty poo, it will smile at you and a little beaming sun will appear next to it. If you've just lost a game, given it an injection or smacked it, it will sulk and moan with a little storm cloud next to it. But in general, the best way to find out exactly what's going on with it is to check the Health Meter. The Health Meter icon is on the bottom of the screen in between the Cleaning icon (a little duck) and the Discipline icon (an angry circle with a chunk cut out of it). Use the A button to illuminate the Health Meter icon, and then select it with B.

You will now be treated to several reports that keep you updated on your egglet's well-being. The first will tell you its age and weight. Your pet's age will be expressed in virtual years, each of which lasts as long as an Earth day. The way of measuring weight depends on where you bought your egglet. Some countries use grams (for example: '5g'), some use pounds (for example: '5lb') while others say ounces (for example: '5oz'). I'm going to use ounces every time I mention it in this book, but your pet might use one of the other measurements. It doesn't make any difference either way, because it's only virtual weight, so it doesn't really matter how we count it.

There were a few problems in 1997 when tamagotchi on sale in the United Kingdom found their way to France. A few French egglet owners got confused by the ounce/gram business, and stuffed their tamagotchi silly with Snacks to try and beef their weight up. Luckily the mistake was spotted in time, and the tamagotchi were given a long exercise to bring their weight down before they became ill from overeating.

The next screen shows the Discipline Meter, which will be blank when your egglet is first born. Your tamagotchi's Discipline Meter will go up each time you punish it, and down each time it gets angry. An extremely well-behaved egglet will have a full Discipline Meter, and a naughty one will have a blank Discipline Meter, but that's no reason to smack your pet around just to fill up the meter. You should let your egglet do whatever it likes until it does something naughty (and *then* smack it). If you smack it without reason it will just get confused, and it won't be able to tell right from wrong. (See Virtual Naughtiness.)

After Discipline comes the Hungry Monitor, which consists of four little hearts. If they're full then your egglet is full too. If they're empty then your egglet is hungry. Some foreign egglet owners have told me they find this a little bit confusing. The Hungry Monitor had a different name in the original Japanese tamagotchi. In Japan, it was the 'Onaka' (Stomach) Monitor, so the fuller the onaka was, the fuller your tamagotchi was. But foreign tamagotchi have the word Hungry written where the Onaka should be, which has led a few people to think that a full Hungry Monitor actually means their tamagotchi is desperate for food. Well, that's not it, it's the other way round, OK? (Anyway, if your egglet is hungry, turn to Feeding Time for further details.)

Finally, there's the Happy Monitor. Like the Hungry Monitor, this consists of four hearts which are initially empty. It's in your interest to keep your egglet happy, because a tamagotchi in a bad mood demands more attention, causes more trouble and will also have a shorter lifespan. Things that cheer your egglet up include feeding it Snacks and playing games with it. (See Feeding Time and Playtime.)

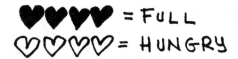

Once your egglet is up and about, remember to lavish it with care and attention. You might be a little surprised at first, because a baby egglet doesn't look in the least bit like the picture on the box. A baby tamagotchi looks like a little black lump with eyes, bouncing around the screen. As with any important stage in your egglet's life, the best thing to do is to check the Health Meter. For a virtual pet's first day on Earth, anything below 10oz is a reasonable weight. Anything above that and it's heading for the fat frontier and could do with a bit of exercise. You will also notice that your egglet is probably hungry and unhappy. First impressions are very important, so make sure that it knows it's being welcomed into a happy, healthy family. Stuff it silly with food, and play with it until all four Happy Hearts are full. After that, you can leave it for a while so it can get used to its new surroundings.

You will probably have noticed that the Discipline Monitor on a baby egglet's Health Meter is completely blank, and that's exactly what it should be. Don't make the mistake that my friend Rei made with her first

tamagotchi. She did all the right things when it hatched, she made sure it was well-fed and happy, but then she saw that the Discipline Monitor wasn't full. So she pressed the Discipline button a few times, which is a horrible thing to do. Imagine how her egglet must have felt, popping out into the world, getting smothered with love and then smacked around for no apparent reason. There are times when you cannot avoid giving your egglet a little slap on the wrist (see Virtual Naughtiness) but you need a good reason. So ignore that Discipline Meter until your egglet starts misbehaving. Besides, your egglet will not become better behaved if you just hit it or shout at it. You have to wait until it's naughty so that it understands why you're disciplining it.

Remember that your egglet has to find out about the world it lives in, and that everything it learns it will have to learn from you. If you set down rules early on in its life, it will grow up following them, so it's a good idea to start as you mean to go on, and to treat your egglet kindly and fairly. Perhaps this is a good time to point out that young tamagotchi will need a lot of care and attention. If you treat them properly, they'll grow up into happy creatures, but even an adult, self-reliant egglet was a lonely baby egglet at some point in its life. Several new tamagotchi owners have made the mistake of hatching their egglet at the wrong time. And by that I mean wrong for the owner, not wrong for the tamagotchi. It's not just people like my brother Ken hatching their tamagotchi before they've learned how to take care of it, some of us also make the mistake of rushing in too fast without thinking of our schedules.

Bearing in mind that young tamagotchi need a lot of attention, make sure that you will be around to give it to them. The best time to hatch a tamagotchi is during the holidays or at the beginning of the weekend. Positively the worst time to hatch one is at about eight o'clock on Monday morning. Your poor egglet will spend most of the day bleating and bleeping, and you'll probably have other things on your mind

like going to school or running a large corporation. (In the event that you find yourself in such a position, see Out and About with Your Pet for a few hints on how to cope.)

FEEDING TIME

The first icon you encounter on the egglet screen is the Feeding icon, which looks like a little knife and fork. You would think, wouldn't you, that for a Japanese toy it should be a little pair of chopsticks, but tamagotchi are international pets and so we use an international symbol for eating food. There are two kinds of food that tamagotchi have to choose from, and

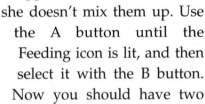

the wise egglet owner will make sure she doesn't mix them up. Use the A button until the Feeding icon is lit, and then select it with the B button. Now you should have two choices on the screen in front of you: Meal and Snack. Use the A button again to select the one you want, and then B to feed your egglet.

Meals

The staple diet of any egglet is a Meal. Four Meals in a row, and your egglet is completely stuffed. Even if all the Hunger lights on the Health Meter are out when it starts eating, four Meals will leave it feeling very satisfied. Tamagotchi don't mind Meals, but they won't start doing cartwheels about them either, if you know what I mean. But Meals are vital for keeping your egglet healthy so make sure it's well-fed. Each Meal you feed a tamagotchi looks like a little loaf of bread, and ought to light one of the hearts on the Hunger Monitor. So even if your egglet's literally starving, four Meals should be enough. Each Meal will also add to your tamagotchi's weight at a rate of 1oz per feeding. Don't worry about this, tamagotchi will naturally put on weight, and in the early stages of their lives you can expect them to put on about 10oz a day.

Snacks

But tamagotchi simply love Snacks. The problem with Snacks is that they don't satisfy hunger and they're very fattening. Every Snack a tamagotchi eats will add 2oz in weight, but your egglet will still be hungry. My brother Ken once spent ages absolutely stuffing his tamagotchi

with Snacks and didn't realize that he was just creating more problems. He ended up with a great big fat egglet in a bad mood, and it was *still* hungry.

Tamagotchi owners have to be very careful how they deal with Snacks. Feeding your egglet a Snack is definitely going to cheer it up; just check the Health Meter before and after to see it's a whole heart happier for every Snack you give it. In fact, Ken says it's possible to keep a tamagotchi alive for a couple of weeks by never playing games with it and just feeding it loads of Snacks. But what you end up with is a very heavy egglet (sometimes up to 99oz at only four days old) who gets ill very easily. Virtual pets can never weigh more than 99oz, and they ought to settle down at that weight when they're about ten. If, say, you're feeding it ten Meals a day, and two Snacks, then playing with it four times a day (which isn't that often when you think about it), that makes:

10 Meals at 1oz per Meal	=	+10oz
2 Snacks at 2oz per Snack	=	+4oz
	=	weight gain of 14oz, minus
4 games at -1oz per game	=	weight loss of 4oz
	=	net weight gain per day of 10oz. Nice and healthy.

That's a perfectly acceptable way to rear a virtual pet. Compare this to Ken's tamagotchi, which he never played with, which refuses to eat proper Meals very often, and always stuffs itself silly with sweets:

2 Meals at 1oz per Meal	=	2oz
10 Snacks at 2oz per Meal	=	20oz
	=	weight gain of 22oz, minus
0 games at -1oz per game	=	weight loss of 0oz
	=	net weight gain per day of 22oz. Lard city.

You don't need to be a mathematical genius to see that Ken's tamagotchi, if treated this way, will reach full adult weight after only five human days! And, naturally, it will be in a permanent bad mood because even though it eats lots of Snacks, it's still always hungry. I wouldn't hold out much hope for Ken's tamagotchi. I'd guess it would keel over and die before its tenth birthday.

But these are just two examples from an infinite number of possibilities. Do try a few experiments, because different combinations and patterns will produce different kinds of adult tamagotchi.

It's important to realize that Snacks are no substitute for the love and affection tamagotchi get from playing

games. Tamagotchi love Snacks so much that nobody could ever ban them from the home entirely, but they need more than just Snacks to keep them happy. Don't get into the habit of throwing your pet a Snack every time you've neglected it, because it will start to expect treats more and more of the time.

I personally try and limit my egglet to one treat a day, which makes it unremarkable, but also untroublesome. If it's feeling particularly depressed, after it's had the flu for example, I might give it a little Snack. I'd also be sure to reward my egglet if it's been quiet when I'm busy. Some tamagotchi owners try and use Snacks to buy their tamagotchi's love, and that's very bad. It encourages the egglet to believe that anyone can behave as badly as they like as long as they hand sweets out at the end, and that simply isn't true.

There is another positive use for Snacks, and that's for helping your egglet to put on weight. If your tamagotchi has been exercising too much (see Playtime) or has just got over a nasty cold (see Virtual Illnesses) you might find that it's a little underweight. A thin egglet might waste completely away, so that might be a good occasion to lard it up a little, by giving it a few Snacks.

Finally on the subject of Snacks, they can be useful as quick and quiet substitutes for playing with your egglet (see Out and About with Your Pet). Playing a game with your tamagotchi can be a very noisy affair, and might get you into trouble in certain places (such as school assembly or meetings with foreign diplomats). But throwing your egglet a Snack will only create a maximum of four little beeps (one to select Feeding, one to open the Feeding menu, one to select Snack, and one to feed it), and so it can be very handy in getting you out of a tight spot.

Your Feeding Questions Answered

One of the questions that people ask me more than any other is 'Bron, how often should I feed my

egglet?' They worry that somehow they're bad virtual parents if their pet doesn't have a full stomach 24 hours a day. Some even try and wake their tamagotchi up in the middle of the night, just to feed it and keep it full!* Opinions are still divided about the pros and cons of feeding times, but as usual, I think that common sense is always the best rule to follow. Although there's nothing wrong with checking on your egglet every ten minutes to make sure it's not a tiny bit peckish, such behaviour might eventually backfire. Your egglet will come to expect to be full all the time, and no doubt you'll be paying it more attention than it really needs. Before long your egglet will be spoilt rigid, and you'll have to discipline it more than you'd like to. So, my advice if you want to feed it all the time is go ahead, but you must be prepared to devote a lot, and I mean *a lot*, of time to your pet. If you want to rear a tamagotchi in this manner, it's

*A waste of time, by the way. You can't wake up a sleeping tamagotchi.

best to do it during your holidays when you know you'll have the time. It can also be rewarding, because a tamagotchi who has enjoyed that much attention is likely to blossom into a very special pet indeed.

Otherwise, I recommend that you get your egglet into the habit of eating at the same time as you do. Instead of feeding it little top-up meals throughout the day, hit the Meal button as many times as it takes to fill its little stomach. If you try and feed it more than its tiny tummy can hold it will simply shake its head to tell you that it doesn't have enough space left. But even if your egglet is completely stuffed, it will always make space for a few Snacks. They're funny like that.

If you're following Bronwen's regular eating policy, you'll normally have to feed it two or three Meals a time. Just count the number of empty hearts on the Health Monitor before mealtime starts and that will tell you all you need to know. It'll wake up each morning feeling a bit hungry, so give it a hearty Meal breakfast when you have yours. Feed it Meals again at lunch-time, again when you have your dinner in the evening, and perhaps even a little Snack before bedtime. Not only will this stop an overfed egglet from pestering you when you're busy, it'll also help you train yourself to feed it regularly. Tamagotchi can't feed themselves, so your pet will be relying on you. Eating together is a good way of ensuring that neither of you forget.

PLAYTIME

Tamagotchi love to play, and the more you play with them the happier they'll be.

On a tamagotchi, the Play icon is the little bat and ball at the top of the screen. As you can see, it's a baseball bat because baseball is an extremely popular sport in Japan, and it's also fun. Most Japanese sports, like sumo (fat people grunt and slap each other), kendo (thin people scream and smack each other with sticks) and judo (the 'gentle art' where you have to hurl each other at the ground) tend to be a little on the violent side, so baseball is a bit more relaxing. To play with your tamagotchi, use the A button to highlight the Play icon, and then select it with B. Your happy egglet will smother you with love for even suggesting a game, and then get down to the serious business of playtime.

But don't think for a moment you'll have to play baseball with your tamagotchi. The game that most tamagotchi like to play is a kind of virtual peekaboo where you have to guess which direction it's going to go in next.

The egglet will wait for you to decide which direction it's going to run. Your choices are Left: A or Right: B. Once you've made your decision, your egglet will reveal its decision. If you were right, that's a plus. If you were wrong, don't worry because you get five chances in each game. If you still can't win the best of five, there's still no problem, because there's nothing to stop you having another game.

Playing games is a great way to keep your egglet happy, even if you're not that good at them. First, your egglet is happy just to get a little attention, so even if you don't play the game very well it will enjoy your company. However, it will love you even more if you're good at the game. The more times you guess correctly, the more you reassure it that you pay so much attention you can actually predict what it's going to do next.

By the way, at the end of each game the tamagotchi will show you the score out of five. The icon it uses to represent itself is a little baby egglet, but the icon it uses to represent you is a big loving heart. They can be so sweet, can't they?

Now here's a top tip from Bronwen for you to keep to yourself, which might make your tamagotchi-rearing life a lot easier. It's an *extremely* good idea to try and look for egglet behaviour patterns. My first ever

tamagotchi was called Migi (which is Japanese for 'right') because most of the time you could guarantee he'd run to the right. So I won nearly every game, he was really easy to keep happy, and we got on fine. It's also a good idea to get a rhythm going with your egglet. It will make little noises as it decides which direction to go. It's possible that each of those noises means it's just turned its head in a new direction, so if you can listen for the right moment you may be able to know exactly which way your egglet is facing.

With Migi I could just keep my finger on the B button and know I'd win most of the time. In fact, I didn't even need to look at the screen while I was playing. Even if your egglet goes left and right equal amounts of time, sometimes it pays off to just keep your finger on one button rather than switch around between A and B. After all, don't forget that you only need to get three out of five guesses to win each game, and by the law of averages, keeping your finger on a single button will reduce your risk to a simple 50/50 chance of winning!

Ken's come up with a tip of his own, which might not always work. He says that if you are playing the peekaboo game with your egglet and you lose the first two guesses, you have a choice. You do what I would do and keep playing, hoping that you win the next three in the row. Or you could follow Ken's advice and just hit the C button to cancel the game. If you do that after losing twice in a row, the Happy Monitor ought to go up by one heart. I have to say that I don't trust Ken on this one because I think he's missing the point.

Knowing him, his tamagotchi was simply happier because it got some attention. Ken's pet was probably so bored that it couldn't care less whether Ken won the game or not. In other words, it was just pleased to see him.

If you try some of these tips on your first egglet and they don't work, don't give up. Tamagotchi have different personalities and you may find that your next egglet fits the bill perfectly. So it's always worth giving these tricks a try when you're rearing a new pet.

As tamagotchi get older, their characters can change. When Migi was five, he went through a brief and difficult phase when he spent more time running to the left, but he soon settled down again. Keep an eye on your egglet and watch to see if there's a pattern you can spot. If you do notice your egglet's own little quirks, you can impress it all the more.

The newer tamagotchi (series #2) prefer to play a different kind of game, in which they will think of a number and you have to guess whether the next number will be higher or lower. The same rules apply as with the left–right game, and if your egglet does follow a particular pattern, it may be even easier for you to spot if it plays the numbers game.

If you have a particularly nasty egglet (which you shouldn't if you're paying attention!) who is badly behaved, spoilt on Snacks and starved of affection, you may start to suspect that he's cheating during some of the games. It's difficult to know how to deal with this problem; the only thing I can recommend is Discipline, but the chances are quite high that if your egglet is that badly behaved, it'll be too late to make much difference.

Playtime with a tamagotchi is more than a mere game. It is also a handy source of exercise for your virtual pet. Each time you play the best-out-of-five game with a tamagotchi, it will run around the screen so much that it will lose 1oz in weight. Watch out especially when your egglet is young (under 10oz in weight) because if you play with it too much without giving it more food, you may tire the poor little thing out. (If you're worried about your egglet's weight, see Feeding Time for the pros and cons of Meals and Snacks.)

VIRTUAL POO

My brother Ken likes to tell foreign tourists that the Japanese have a saying: 'All things must poo.' Well, let me tell you that the only Japanese who ever said that was my brother Ken, and that's only because he likes to annoy people. None the less, there's no avoiding it, for once in his life my brother is absolutely right. And tamagotchi, like any other life form be they virtual or real, do have to go to the toilet every now and then.

Fortunately for the world at large, one of the advantages of virtual poo is that it doesn't smell. In fact, it's very easy for a careless egglet owner not to notice that anything has happened. The egglet won't tell you if it's popped out a parcel on the nice clean virtual floor, it'll just stand there and look at it. I suppose that the sight of a turd makes for a nice change of scene if you're a tamagotchi. It's one of the reasons that you can't just rely on the egglet to bleep when it needs something; you will have to pick it up every now and then and have a look. It's very easy to see if your egglet has gone to the toilet, because there will be a large, steaming pile of poo sitting right there on your screen.

Now ordinarily, you might think this is the ideal moment to discipline your egglet, but it's important not to because your egglet has no choice. It has to go to the toilet, and that's the only place it can do it, so there's no point in going mad. Don't smack it, it's only doing what comes naturally. If you're going to share your life with a tamagotchi, expect to clean up egglet turds at least once or twice a day.

In order to clean up after your tamagotchi, you'll need to select the Duck icon. A lot of foreign tamagotchi owners believe there must be some kind of explanation rooted deep in the Japanese past – some old story about a magical toilet-cleaning duck for example. But there isn't. Some have suggested it's the kind of rubber duck you might find in a bath. But actually, it's a picture of a Japanese potty for little kids, which is sometimes made in the shape of a duck to try and encourage children to sit on them more often. Just select the icon and press B to see something that looks like a large zigzaggy brush sweep the tamagotchi poo away. It's not actually a brush, it's supposed to be a big clean wave that flushes across the screen.

Some breeds of egglet may smile and jump around a bit, but not because they're happy the turd has gone (it doesn't seem to bother them that much). My brother Ken has this theory that tamagotchi like surfing on the wave as it washes across the screen, but I think they're just pleased to see that you're checking up on them. Ken did try tricking his egglet by clicking the Duck icon when there was no poo around, but it didn't seem very impressed.

It's important to clear up egglet poo as soon as possible because tamagotchi can get ill if they're left in all that mess for too long (see Virtual Illnesses). One of Ken's favourite experiments was waiting to see just how much poo could collect on the screen before trouble started, and he reckons you can get up to eight turds up there at once. But even a happy egglet will start to notice that many, because it's harder for them to move around when they have to tiptoe around large steaming piles of poo. Eight poos on the screen will mean, in most cases, that your egglet is invisible behind a huge pile of it, and that it is likely to get very ill, very quickly.

VIRTUAL ILLNESSES

Everybody gets ill from time to time, and that includes tamagotchi. You'll know your egglet is sick because a black skull will appear in the top right-hand corner of the screen. It may get unhappy very fast, and be unwilling to play games or eat food.

To help your egglet get well, you'll have to give it a little injection. Use the A button to select the syringe icon

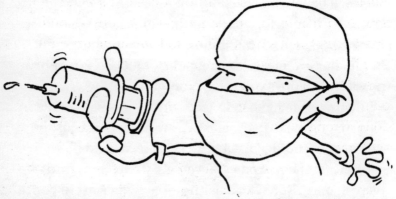

at the top right corner of the screen and then give your tamagotchi a shot by pressing B. If it's seriously ill, you may have to give it more than one injection, so instead of sitting around wondering what to do when you see that skull, my advice is to move as fast as possible. Tamagotchi have mixed feelings about injections. A virtual needle hurts a tamagotchi as much as a real one would hurt you or me, so tamagotchi always moan a little bit. However, a smart, well-behaved egglet will also realize that the injection has cured its sickness, so it will be quite happy. I recommend that you give your egglet a Snack once it's had its injection, otherwise it might think that you're punishing it for something it can't control.

Ken came up with a nasty little scheme for his egglet. He told me that he could stop it from ever getting ill by giving it several injections a day as a kind of vaccination, but I found out soon enough that he was just looking for an excuse to cause trouble. First, the injections only work when the egglet is ill, so stuffing it full of injections will only turn it into an angry pin cushion. But second, a smart egglet will simply refuse to have an injection if it isn't ill. So Ken's just lying again, as usual.

A lot of people come to me and say: 'Bron! What have I done wrong? I've kept my

tamagotchi well-fed, I always clean up its poo the moment it appears, I go easy on the Snacks and I play with it all the time. So why does it still get ill?' Well, all I can say is that tamagotchi get colds just like anyone else, and they're especially vulnerable when they're young. You can't wrap them up in virtual cotton wool and expect them to live a life that's completely free of disease. I remember the time my first tamagotchi, Migi, got the tamagotchi flu. He was only a year old and I thought that somehow I'd been a bad tamagotchi owner. I burst into tears and ran to my dad and asked him what had happened. But he reminded me that it's nobody's fault when you get ill. So if your tamagotchi gets a cold, don't panic, it's not because of something you've done wrong. But it will be if your tamagotchi still has a cold a few hours later, because you should have been checking up. Give your tamagotchi an injection the moment you see that it's sick, and the problem should pass quite quickly.

BEDTIME

Any egglet owner will tell you that their virtual pet is as cute as a cute thing that just won the Cutest thing in Cuteland competition. And to keep bright and perky, your egglet will need its beauty sleep.

A young egglet normally goes to bed around eight o'clock, although as they get older they'll want to stay up later. The naughty ones can get into the habit of going to bed as late as ten! When a young tamagotchi decides it's time for bed, it will just go to sleep and start snoring. If your tamagotchi is older, it will roll out a little futon, which is a Japanese bed that goes on the floor, and sleep right there in the middle of the screen. Just before it dozes off, it will beep a goodnight at you, and then it'll be dreaming of Snacks and Playtime until the next day.

Your main duty as a tamagotchi owner is to turn out the light so that your egglet gets a better night's sleep. You can do this by selecting the Light bulb icon with the A button and then calling up the Light bulb menu by pressing B.

You will find two choices, ON and OFF, and all you have to do is select OFF with A and then click the switch by pressing B. They can sleep with the light on, but they won't be quite as well rested and they might be a little crotchety the following day. Also, the later you leave the light on after your egglet's gone to sleep, the later your egglet will want to go to bed once it's older. You find yourself going to bed before your egglet does, which will mean that it will be even naughtier and nastier the following day because you weren't there to tuck it in.

One thing worth remembering is that a sleeping egglet is dead to the world, so make sure you've done everything you want to do before it goes to bed. You can't feed it, play with it, give it an injection or clear up any poo once it's asleep, so everything has to wait until the following morning. I remember one terrible time we all went to the cinema, and because I didn't want to get in trouble during the movie, I left Migi at home. When I came home I found that he had already gone to bed. He was very hungry, not particularly happy and was sleeping next to a giant poo that he must have done while I was out. Luckily, no harm was done and I made a big fuss of him the next morning, but just think what might have happened if he'd gone to bed with the flu or something like that!

Bronwen's top tip for happy bedtimes is to make a point of checking up on your egglet about fifteen minutes before it's likely to go to sleep. Feed it if it's hungry, play with it until its Happy Monitor has four full hearts, and do any cleaning up that has to be done. That way your egglet will go to bed happy and content, and have a peaceful night's sleep.

Tamagotchi need about twelve hours sleep, but a well-behaved egglet won't cause any trouble the next morning when it wakes up. It'll just switch its light on and start scampering around the screen as usual. It won't bother you unless it's really hungry or unhappy, and if you made a fuss over it just before bedtime it should be quiet and content well into the morning. Perhaps now you can see why it's so important to make sure the clock shows the right time (see Hatching), because even the most well-behaved egglet has no way of knowing if its clock is right. Ken's badly behaved tamagotchi woke him up in the night because the poor little thing thought it was midday and that everyone would be awake. Well, we were awake once it started beeping, but we weren't very happy about it, I can tell you.

By the way, here's something you might want to try once you're an experienced tamagotchi owner. Hatch a tamagotchi with less than an hour to go before bedtime. That way it'll still be in the baby stage (see The Tamagotchi Life Cycle) when it goes to sleep, and instead of changing into the next stage after 60 minutes, it will have a whole night's sleep as a baby before it begins growing. This can be very, very good for a tamagotchi, but you'll need to be a well-practiced tamagotchi owner before you can really reap the benefits in later life.

VIRTUAL NAUGHTINESS

One of the most difficult times for the good egglet owner comes when your egglet starts misbehaving. Of course, if you're my little brother Ken then you love it, because you've got a great excuse to hit the poor little thing, but if you're a kind-hearted soul like me, you'll be worried about hurting it.

The trouble is, sometimes you have to be cruel to be kind. If your egglet is naughty and you don't punish it, then it will keep being naughty. Bad-mannered little tamagotchi will grow up into bad-mannered big tamagotchi. They'll cheat at games, they'll pester you when you're busy, they'll demand more and more Snacks and then refuse to play with you if you don't give in. They might even start pooing on the floor for fun, not

realizing that they might make themselves ill. Then you have to cure them with an injection that will hurt them, and that will make them even nastier and even more demanding.

So, no matter how much you love your egglet, at some point you will have to take a deep breath and smack it. It will probably hurt you more than it hurts your egglet, but you just have to grit your teeth and get on with it. Disciplining your egglet is quite easy to do, in fact, a little too easy. Most of the icons on your screen will take you to a menu where you have to make other choices, but the Discipline icon will smack your tamagotchi the moment you press B to select it. Sometimes it's all too easy to hit that B button without thinking. One of Ken's favourite excuses is that he was going to check up on his tamagotchi with the Health Meter (whose icon is the one before Discipline on the screen) but accidentally pressed the button one time too many. So instead of getting the Health Meter, he presses Discipline and whacks his tamagotchi. Watch out for that one because it's an easy mistake to make, although Ken makes it so often he's either stupid or lying. (Knowing Ken, it's probably a bit of both.)

So, how do you know when your egglet is misbehaving? This is a very important question, because sometimes the answer will depend on how you have treated your egglet in the past. The first sign is probably (but only *probably*, mind you) when you try to feed or play with the egglet but instead it stands there and shakes its head. The most common sign of tamagotchi naughtiness is refusing to eat or refusing to play a game, but before you whack it it's crucial to check the Health Meter. Have a look at the egglet's weight, and make sure that it isn't unhappy or fully fed. A tamagotchi will naturally refuse to eat any more food if it's already full, so that's not naughtiness, that's a stuffed and happy egglet telling you that it's had enough, thank you very much. A tamagotchi will refuse to play with you if it's tired out, so try and remember if you've been playing with it a lot recently.

Sure-fire signs of a naughty egglet are:
- Refusing to eat when you know it's hungry
- Refusing to play when you know it's not completely happy
- Beeping for attention when it is neither hungry nor unhappy

There are times when Discipline is not quite as clear cut. Let's suppose that you've been rather busy recently, and you haven't had much of a chance to play with your tamagotchi. You haven't given it any Snacks either so it's actually feeling rather depressed and lonely. But then it gets the tamagotchi flu, and you know that you simply must give it an injection to avoid further complications.

But when you try to give your tamagotchi an injection, it solemnly shakes its head and sulks.

It might be scared, or it might be in a bad mood; either way you have to smack it before it will let you give it the medicine it needs. You might possibly be able to bribe it with a Snack, but you know how I feel about using Snacks as substitutes for sensible egglet parenting. Shame on you. And if the Snack bribery still doesn't work, you have no choice except to smack it, but to be honest, the only person who should be getting a smack is you because it's your fault that your egglet is too angry to take its medicine. We Japanese take that kind of thing very seriously. As a tamagotchi owner you have to be your pet's foster parent, and if you fail in your duties you will be dishonoured. But hopefully, you'll never find yourself in that position. If you do, be sure to make it up to your egglet with plenty of games to cheer it up.

My brother Ken, I might add, is one of the most dishonourable people in the world. I'm quite sure that he deliberately tries to make his tamagotchi sick. In ancient Japan, people like him were hung upside down with their head in a bucket of tomato soup until they admitted the errors of their ways. That's what Dad told me anyway.

OUT AND ABOUT
WITH YOUR PET

Virtual pets are happy little creatures that live inside a little plastic bubble full of electronic parts. If their owner is a kind and well-rounded person (in other words, if their owner is anyone except my brother Ken) they don't really have very much to worry about. However, human beings like you and me are big creatures that live on planet Earth with five billion other creatures, and owning a virtual pet can cause all sorts of problems. Don't expect everyone else you meet to be as keen on them as you are. Many will regard your pet as little more than an alarm clock that can't be set properly, and in this world of mobile phones and overhead jets, others will simply think the sound of happy beeping is an annoying distraction. You also need to worry about your pet's safety, not just from other people, but also from natural dangers.

Egglets Outside

Perhaps the most practical concern of the sensible owner is how to ensure your pet is safe and sound when you take it out of the house. I like to carry mine hanging on one of my belt loops so I don't have to root around in my pockets if it needs attention. But if you want to do the same, make sure that you secure it safely. When you first get a tamagotchi, it'll probably have a little chain with a kind of clip so you can fasten and unfasten it. The original Japanese chain was a bit fragile, and although the chain's been strengthened for the foreign versions, I still don't recommend that you rely on it to hold your pet in place. The fastener can be difficult to open and close at first, but quickly becomes loose and untrustworthy. Many of the pets I have reared on the farm have been brought to me by neighbours who found them lying in the street with a broken chain. Luckily, most of the owners knew my reputation and came to collect their lost pets, but you don't really want to find yourself in the same position.

For my egglets, I normally get some cord or a stronger chain with a better fastener, and thread it through the strong metal ring at the top of the casing. That way, I know my pet will be secure. If you want to carry yours on your keyring, I think it's good idea to use this method too. If I have to go to a party or somewhere else where I need to wear a nice dress, I wear it on a necklace, which is a trick I recommend to any girls out there. If you're a boy and you're wearing a dress to a party, then you're in trouble.

There are many other forms of outdoor egglet wear. Ken tried to convince my friend Rei that she'd look good with egglet earrings, but she realized what was going on when he came round to her place with a pointy chopstick and offered to pierce them for her. Even if it hadn't been Ken's idea, I would have thought it was a silly idea because while virtual pets weigh nothing in the real world, the casing weighs quite a bit and can be rather heavy on the ears. Rei also tried threading a bracelet through the ring on the casing and wearing it on her wrist, but it kept getting in the way.

Weirder forms of virtual pet fashion include the egglet loafer, where the chain is woven into your shoelaces. I think this is a terrible idea, not only because all that bouncing about is liable to damage your egglet's delicate insides, but also because you'd have to be a circus performer to reach it if it needs attention.

Some people like to hang their virtual pets on the outside of their bags. This is fine as long as you follow my warning about the chain, but I advise against it if you go to school or any other situation when you are likely to find yourself in the company of criminals. A pet on your belt is always in view and ready-to-hand, but if it's hanging from a bag over your shoulder, it's just asking to get swiped by a thief.

Generally speaking, the most sensible place to keep your pet is in your pocket, but I've noticed that it can be difficult to hear it if it bleeps in your pocket when you're walking down a city street. So be sure to check up on it regularly.

Egglets at School

A common worry I hear from my friends is how you can look after your virtual pet at times when you've got duties that take you away from home. Possibly the most trying time for a pet-lover is the daily trip to school. All kinds of virtual pet make a significant amount of noise, especially when they are playing, and it's only when you're trying to keep yours quiet that you really hear how noisy it can be. In Japan there's not too much of a problem, because egglet owners have got their pets well trained, and usually manage to ensure they get all the

attention they require between lessons, during break times, and during the lunch hour. But if you're new to virtual pet-rearing, you might still have to check up on yours in the presence of authority figures (such as your teacher, company chairman or prison warder) who will not appreciate it.

The easy answer is simply to turn the sound off. On a tamagotchi you can do this by pressing the C button. While still holding the C button, also press the A button to hear a little double-beep sound. Your tamagotchi is now in stealth mode, and won't make a sound until you perform the same operation to restore it. But stealth mode won't solve all of your problems. First, you'll have to look at your egglet much more frequently, because you won't hear it at all if it needs attention. But second, you'll still need to press those buttons, and some people (like the person trying to teach you geography in school) may take offence if they catch you at it.

Of course, you could always just take out your virtual pet and play with it, but remember that there's more at risk than simple confiscation. If your pet is taken away from you, it will be in the hands of someone who probably doesn't know how to look after it properly. You won't be able to play with it, feed it, give it medicine or clear up any mess, and your egglet will end up feeling neglected and unloved.

If tamagotchi are new in your neighbourhood, you can probably get away with Ken Komatsubara's patent 'benri benjo' method. The benri benjo (or 'beneficial bog') routine involves a sudden and desperate desire to go to the toilet, during which you can then check up on your pet without interference. However, this does have several drawbacks, the most unpleasant of which was discovered by Ken when he accidentally dropped his down the toilet. Another problem with Ken's rather fiendish (and for him, unusually clever) scam is that it will only work for a limited amount of time. Once everybody else has got a virtual pet, your teacher will start to get a bit suspicious when the entire class fakes a mass outbreak of the squirts

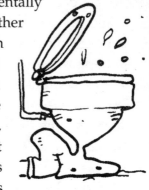

every single day. You can probably stretch the benri benjo routine for a couple more days by handing over your pets to a trusted member of the class who can take them all off for secret feeding, but your teacher will eventually work out that something fishy is going on. The other problem is that the sounds of a virtual pet beeping tend to echo round the average toilet, and the noise can carry right down the corridor to passing teachers. So this is definitely a good time to turn the sound off.

Egglets in Public

If your pet starts bleating for attention in a public place and you can't get it into stealth mode, you might find yourself in considerable trouble. I have tried experimenting with muffling the sounds but I haven't found a satisfactory way. You can try and operate it without taking it out of your pocket, but that won't mask all the noise and you run a serious risk of hitting the wrong button by accident. The other way is to try and hold it in such a way as to cover up the bit that makes the noise, but since virtual pets don't have a speaker thingy as such, but seem to emit noise from all over, such a method is doomed to failure.

Japanese kimonos have pockets in their sleeves, and it's possible to keep your hands and pet hidden inside your sleeves while operating it. It still makes a noise, but if you're standing in a crowd then no one can be sure that the sound is coming from you. However, to do this trick you need to be a Japanese girl, wearing a kimono and standing with at least forty other Japanese girls, which is OK for me, but probably a bit more difficult if you're you.

Egglets in Summertime

Inside the casing of your egglet it's virtual summer all year round, but during real-world summer be sure you don't leave it lying around in the heat. Going to the beach can be murder for the virtual pet owner, especially if you are in the company of my brother Ken, who enjoys nothing better than burying

things in the sand. But a caring egglet owner spending a day at the beach will know that they can't simply leave their electronic buddy at home. I recommend sealing it in a little plastic bag to keep out water, sand and sun lotion. It will probably be difficult to hear it beeping for attention, so you'll need to check up on it regularly, but you can operate the A, B and C buttons through the bag, so it ought to guarantee that your pet remains safe and sound. Watch out for the greenhouse effect, though. Your egglet will bake even faster if left inside a plastic bag underneath a hot sun, so make sure you always keep it in the shade.

Egglets in Wintertime

Winter travel requires a similar amount of care for the needs of your pet. The middle of Japan is packed with mountains that are very good for skiing, but going out in the snow can be very troublesome, especially if Ken is busy shovelling snow down the back of your neck. To avoid damage from melting snow, try using the same plastic bag trick. The bag will also help insulate your egglet from the cold, but I advise you not to take any chances. All electrical items are at risk from extreme changes in temperature, so do try and keep it snug, preferably by carrying it in an inner pocket of your coat.

Egglet Confusion

One final point on egglets away from home, and that's the crucial issue of telling them apart. There are many styles of casing, but not *that* many, and the chances are quite high that you and at least one of your friends will have the same colour and design. My brother Ken is all in favour of scratching your initials into the back of the casing, but I think that's a little dangerous. Besides, why should your egglet have a less than perfect casing, purely because others may not be able to tell it apart from their own? Perhaps a few spangly stickers on the casing, or a ribbon through the chain ring is the answer.*

*Editor's note: Not recommended for company presidents, gangster rappers and military personnel.

BABY-SITTERS

Rearing a virtual pet is a rewarding but complicated business, and any serious owner is likely to become very attached to their new-found friend. Just how attached you are normally becomes clear the first time someone asks if they can look at your pet themselves. You may find yourself handing it over proudly, and beaming at

them while they examine your pet, then suddenly going mad when your innocent human friend goes anywhere near the buttons. That is normally the moment when the average egglet owner panics, and realizes that they don't really trust anyone else with their beloved pet.

Everybody has their own style of egglet-rearing, and the presence of another individual can be quite unsettling. It doesn't matter if they're a saint, a professor or a rock star, any good egglet owner is going to be a bit nervous about other people's fingers on those switches.

You start to worry if they're going to press the Discipline button by accident, annoy your pet by playing games in a different way, or even feed it too many Snacks and cause you problems down the line. If your friend is known to be a fellow pet-lover, then it's normally easier to leave yours in their care, but even the kindest-hearted owner is likely to get a little bit fidgety when someone else goes near their pet.

Just imagine how much worse it can be for the egglet owner when they are forced to leave their prized possession with someone else for an extended period of time. But it's almost certain that baby-sitters are going to get involved in your life at some point. Possibly your school will issue a blanket ban on virtual pets and you don't want to risk losing your tamagotchi to an uncaring teacher. Perhaps you have to go on a trip where you know there's no chance whatsoever that your virtual pet is going to get the love and attention it requires. Whatever happens, you will have to pick the best of a bad bunch and find someone to look after your egglet for you.

There's a special kind of tamagotchi in Japan that solves this problem for you, but it's unlikely to be something you can easily get hold of. It's called a tamapitchi, and it's a tamagotchi that's built into a real-life mobile phone! If you have to go somewhere you can phone up a friend with their own tamapitchi and send your pet down the phone! Then your friend can baby-sit until you come back, at which point they can phone you and send your tamagotchi back safe and sound. But if you haven't got a tamapitchi, you're still left with the problem of finding a suitable baby-sitter close to hand.

So, whom do you choose? Someone you know, someone you trust, someone with a track record in bringing up virtual pets. But let's face it, the chances of that are pretty remote. The only likely candidate would be a saint or one of your egglet-friendly school friends, and the chances are quite high that you don't know that many saints and that your friends will be going on the same trip as you, and consequently stuck with the same search for a minder.

Instead of a reliable minder, you will be forced to choose second best, so here are my top tips on the different kinds of egglet baby-sitter.

(1) The Harassed Housewife

Look for a mixture of confusion and fear, and eyes that

dart to the side every time the egglet beeps. It's in her pocket and she hopes nobody else can hear the noise. Her child's made her promise to care for 'a pet' but to her it looks just like a digital watch. Junior has spent five minutes trying to explain what all the buttons do, but it's gone in one ear and out the other. Now the busy parent is trying to do the shopping, hoping that the beeping sounds will go away. The egglet in her pocket is probably lonely, hungry and smelly. If it's still there by the time Junior comes back, it will be in a very bad mood indeed.

Bronwen says: More than an hour with this minder, and you'll need a new egglet. Or a new parent.

(2) The Useless Yuppie

Look for a razor-sharp suit, shiny gel in his hair, personal organiser and mobile phone. This is an important business executive who's become an accidental egglet owner because every now and then he gets hold of an office toy to help him stay calm. Maybe he volunteered to look after it for his daughter (and of course, he promised her that he would look after it better than anyone else

I LOVE MY TAMAGOTCHI • 65

because he's a dad and that's his job). Little does he know that, while rearing a virtual pet is a rewarding experience, it is not a time-wasting exercise for bored office workers. He's already got into trouble with his boss, and only managed to cover his tracks by pretending that the noise was his mobile phone. Fellow workers have noticed him rushing off to the toilet more than usual, and the cleaners have reported strange beeping sounds coming from the men's rest-room. He thinks he's god's gift to virtual pets, but his egglet eats too many sweets and doesn't get enough playtime.

Bronwen says: Avoid like the plague. Let your dad spoil *you*, not your tamagotchi.

(3) The Gonk Geek

The first person on your block to get a virtual pet wasn't a schoolgirl or a millionaire, it was the boy next door who spends all day indoors playing with his computer. You can guarantee that he's grown up surrounded by pet rocks, lucky gonks and other weird stuff that has prepared him fully for the spiritually demanding task of egglet-rearing. After a shaky start, he has become quite a dab hand at looking after virtual pets. His pets are always well-behaved and well-loved. Bronwen says:

He might smell a bit, but your egglet is probably in safe hands. Beware wolves in sheep's clothing, some of these boys might be my brother Ken in disguise.

(4) The Office Angel

In Japan we call them Office Ladies or OLs. The patron saints of photocopying, flower-arranging and coffee-making. If I had a big sister, this is probably the job she'd be doing. The OLs were one of the main groups in Japanese society that the tamagotchi were originally designed for, and their reputation for kindness and caring is well-deserved. If your dad is looking after your egglet, in a perfect world he'll give it to a kindly OL.

Bronwen says: You couldn't find a better baby-sitter for your egglet. It'll come back to you with a full stomach and a happy heart.*

(5) The Gormless Granny

Grandparents are suckers for any chance to impress the kids, but don't believe them when they say they can look after your egglet. Forget for a moment that they can't program the video and think that digital watches are

*Editor's note: Bronwen has never been to an office in this country, and so has no idea of the differing standards of secretarial behaviour or that she might get a knuckle sandwich if she tried talking to a secretary here in this manner.

alien invaders. Concentrate instead on the implications of short-sightedness and slight deafness. I SAID SLIGHT DEAFNESS! Do you really want your egglet in the care of someone who may not be able to hear it beeping for attention, see what's wrong or press the buttons to sort the problem out.

Bronwen says: A granny's heart is in the right place, but no one's going to come out of this well. Your egglet's going to be very unhappy, and both you and granny will feel guilty for not predicting the problems in advance.

(6) The Egglet Thief

Every school has big, lumbering stupid kids who enjoy hitting people because they're too thick to get a sensible hobby like flower-arranging. That's the way life is, and in the great scheme of things that is human existence, these unfortunate creatures will grow up to get jobs in management. The school bully will have spent many long hours telling everyone how stupid virtual pets are, although after the first few days of watching the others, he will harbour a desperate, secret desire to have one of his own. However, bullies being bullies, he can't back down and admit he's interested, so he will be on the look out for an excuse to steal someone else's.

Bronwen says: It's possible that the love of a good egglet can transform even the stupidest bully into a kind, enlightened individual. But don't risk your beloved pet to find out. If you let him look after your egglet, you will never see it again.

(7) The Pet Pundit

Everybody knows someone who thinks they are the World's Greatest Expert On Everything. You would hope that egglet-rearing would encourage people to think of other's feelings and just be nice to each other, but the world is full of idiots and one of the most dangerous kinds of idiot is the self-appointed Pet Pundit. He (or she, there are just as many girls who think they know it all) will guarantee that he will look after your egglet well. In fact, he will secretly think that he will do a far better job than you. He will tut and moan about the condition of your egglet, blame any problems on the way you have brought your egglet up, and keep on moaning even after you get your egglet back (if you get it back).

Bronwen says: If a pet pundit tells you they're a world famous egglet expert, nod happily. Tell them that you know they're famous, so famous in fact that you read about them in this book, and that Bronwen said they were a moron. Don't let them anywhere near your pet.

(8) You

Bronwen says: You are the only person in the world who really, truly knows and understands what your egglet wants. Are you really sure you can't take it with you? (See Out and About with Your Pet for a few tips.)

Now for more about my favourite kind of egglet, the tamagotchi. No matter what kind of creature it turns into (and with all the different versions of tamagotchi, these days we're looking at over twenty), there's a kind of family tree they follow, and you can chart both your egglet's progress and your own as a tamagotchi owner. I've drawn up a table to summarize the various kinds of tamagotchi you can currently find, using what information I've been able to glean about breeds #1 and #2. There's a third breed out in Japan, but they shouldn't be much of an issue over here until the middle of 1998 at the earliest. Anyway, we'd better have a look at the different kinds of tamagotchi there are. It's surprising how many you can get.

(1) Egg

The first stage in a tamagotchi's life is the egg stage, which lasts about five minutes from activation to hatching. The egg will have a kind of patchy, speckled surface in the original tamagotchi, although if you have one of the later versions (Tamagotchi #2) the egg will be a uniform dark shade. This, by the way, is also the only time in its life cycle when it is actually a 'tamagotchi'. The other stages have different names in Japanese, which I've mentioned below.

(2) Infant

When your tamagotchi is born it will be a 'babitchi', and it will stay a babitchi for about sixty minutes (unless bedtime comes first, in which case it will sleep as a babitchi and transform the next morning). Many people have argued that all babitchi, like all babies, look exactly the same, and I think they're absolutely right. Only a babitchi's real mother is likely to be able to tell it apart from any other babitchi. Characteristics of the infant tamagotchi are that it has no facial features except for a big pair of googly eyes and a tiny little mouth. The skin is dark, and the tamagotchi will have no legs at this stage, so it will bounce around your screen in a frenzy.

That's the most common form of tamagotchi, although if you are extremely lucky and have one of the new breed it will look slightly different. So if your egg was dark instead of speckled, you will find yourself looking after a shiro-babitchi. 'Shiro' means 'white' so no prizes for guessing what colour it is. The shiro-babitchi is a slightly wobblier version of the babitchi, and is also nicknamed the 'Isaiah' because 'one *eye's higher* than the other'.

The most noticeable thing about the babitchi is that it hardly ever stops eating. Whereas a well-behaved adult tamagotchi only gets really hungry a few times a day, a babitchi will seem to get hungry every few minutes. Don't worry about it, they need plenty of food to grow and they're very energetic. No matter how much you stuff them they won't go above 5oz in weight, until they transform into the next stage. According to my brother Ken, both black and white babitchi are incredibly resilient, and they are literally impossible to kill off at this stage. I dread to think how many times Ken experimented before he was sure of this.

(3) Child

After about an hour of human time, your pet will grow up into a 'marutchi', which is a roundish sort of thing. This is quite handy, because the name is Japanese for 'roundy-thing'. Not surprisingly, this is a bigger, whiter version of the babitchi, still with no legs, and still bouncing happily around the screen. If you're old enough to remember a video game called Pacman, the marutchi will look very familiar, especially when it munches on Meals and Snacks. Your pet will be a marutchi for several tamagotchi years, which is two or three human days.

In the new tamagotchi breeds, it will grow into a 'ton-marutchi', which is much more squashy, has the trademark one eye higher than the other, and also a little nobbly bit on top of its head.

(4) Youth

This is where the business of tamagotchi-rearing starts to get very complicated, because after the childhood stage they can grow into all manner of different creatures. When a tamagotchi is a few human days old, it can change again into two distinct types. In both cases, it will stop bouncing around the screen because it will be too big and heavy. For the first time, you will see your tamagotchi walk! The traditional kind is the 'tamatchi' which is like a marutchi with a pair of spindly arms and cute little legs poking out from underneath it. There is a slightly different kind called a 'kuchitamatchi' which has big sticky-out lips. Although much of your tamagotchi's character and behaviour will be clear by this stage, many tamagotchi owners, especially new ones, take this long to identify their tamagotchi as a distinct individual.

In the new tamagotchi series, this stage also follows on quite logically from what came before. Your ton-marutchi will grow into either a 'tongaritchi' (with a nobbly head and little feet) or a 'hashitamatchi' (which looks like a kuchitamatchi with one eye higher than the other).

(4) Adult

Hope you're not getting cross-eyed at all these Japanese words and descriptions, because it's just about to get even more complicated. In each of the tamagotchi breeds there are six different kinds of adult forms your pet can take. The most common form is the 'ginjirotchi', which looks a little bit like a grinning hippo with a crew cut. The ginjirotchi is the version you're most likely to find in adult tamagotchi if the owner has spent a reasonable amount of time and effort with their pet. However, slight differences in your behaviour towards your pet can result in your tamagotchi growing into several very different forms.

If you've been more neglectful with the injections and with the poo-cleaning, you're likely to find yourself looking at a 'kuchipatchi'. This looks like the lippy kuchitamatchi, with the addition of stumpy little legs. The kuchipatchi isn't particularly naughty, but it is likely to get ill more often than the average tamagotchi, so if your pet grows into one of these expect plenty of hassle with the tamagotchi flu.

If you wake up one morning to find a humanoid figure with black lumps on its head (which could be a strange hairstyle or even little cat ears) then you've just reared yourself a 'mametchi'. These tamagotchi are one of the best you can have, because they've got long lifespans, are normally well-behaved and hardly ever get sick.

However, if you've been lax in your duties, you won't be so lucky. In fact, you might end up with a 'nyorotchi', which is a lippy little head that bounces around on the end of a long tail. These are ungrateful individuals who seem to spend most of their time moaning that they're ill.

The only tamagotchi nastier than that is the 'tarakotchi', which has big lips but spindly legs. The tarakotchi is liable to cheat during games, and is an incessant pest. It will beep for attention all the time, probably because it was spoiled rotten as a child and now thinks that it has a full-time slave instead of an owner.

There's one more kind of adult tamagotchi in the #1 breed, and that's the 'masktchi'. The masktchi is pretty hard to describe. Some people think it looks like a sheep in a Lone Ranger mask, others that it looks like a blob with spindly legs and a very small cat's head. Either way, the masktchi is fun to have around, partially because it's well-mannered and healthy, but mainly because if you've got a masktchi there's a strong chance it will grow up into one of the 'special' tamagotchi. These are very difficult to get because they require you to be a perfect tamagotchi owner from the moment your pet hatches, but if you've got a masktchi on your screen then you're definitely heading in the right direction.

In breed #2 of tamagotchi there are even more complicated names that you have to deal with. Luckily, most of them look quite similar to the breed #1 versions in many cases. For those who want to know exactly which one's which, the smart 'mimitchi' looks like a plumper version of the series #1 mametchi, except in this case the lumps on the head are big enough to look like rabbit ears. The 'potchitchi' looks like a cute little puppy. The 'kusatchi' is a dancing flower in a plant pot (with sticky-out lips). The 'takotchi' is an octopus. Finally, there's the 'hashizotchi', which looks like a fat bird with stubby wings, and the 'zukitchi' which looks like a little devil, or perhaps if you're more artistically-minded, a jellyfish in a jester's hat. Be careful if you find yourself rearing a zukitchi, because they can be very demanding and bullying.

(5) Special

The special stage is something that most tamagotchi owners don't get to see, because in order to see the hidden character in each tamagotchi breed, you have to be one of the best tamagotchi owners in the world. Even if you *are* the best tamagotchi owner in the world, you still might not ever see the special stage, because there's also a certain random element involved. Still, if you played your cards right on the original Japanese version, you might be lucky enough to rear an 'oyajitchi'. This looks like the head of a balding old man with wispy tufts of hair and a little goatee beard, standing on little spindly legs. But you're unlikely to see the oyajitchi outside Japan because this creature was dropped from the export version. Instead, breed #1 tamagotchi outside Japan feature the 'ketotchi' which looks like a blonde man's head, or perhaps a man in a white beret. I'm not too sure what the name is supposed to tell us, bearing in mind that the 'oyaji' of oyajitchi means 'dad', whereas the 'keto' of ketotchi could mean 'hairy foreigner'. I'm sure there's a perfectly good explanation, but I can't think of what it could be. A ketotchi is a bit lazy, likes to stay in bed for most of the morning, and doesn't go to bed till quite late.

The series #2 tamagotchi aren't available outside Japan yet, but if you manage to get your hands on one (and are so amazing that you manage to grow it into the special character), you will see a cute little sumo wrestler with a topknot called a 'sekitoritchi'.

(6) Afterlife

But it doesn't end there, because all tamagotchi, whether you rear them to adulthood or the special character, will eventually pass away into the next life. If you have a Japanese tamagotchi, it will transform into its final stage, the 'obaketchi' which comes from 'obake', meaning 'ghost'. This looks a little like a ghost with a long squiggly tail, and it will wriggle around the screen next to a gravestone with a cross on top. The version available outside Japan is very different. It's an angel-gotchi, which as you might expect, has little wings and flits around with spangly stars in the heavens.

STAGE	DESCRIPTION	BREED
Egg		
Tamagotchi #1	Speckly egg	#1
Tamagotchi #2	Dark egg	#2
Infant		
Babitchi	Black blob with googly eyes	#1
Shiro-babitchi	White blob with 'Isaiah' eyes	#2
Child		
Marutchi	Little round thing like a Pacman	#1
Ton-marutchi	Squashy 'Isaiah' thing with nobbly wotsit on head	#2
Youth		
Kuchitamatchi	Big sticky-out lips	#1
Tamatchi	Little round thing with stumpy legs	#1
Tongaritchi	Same but with nobbly head and no arms	#2
Hashitamatchi	'Isaiah' with sticky out lips	#2

Adult

Kuchipatchi	Lippy thing with fat little legs	#1
Mametchi	Looks like a racoon/girl with buns on head	#1
Ginjirotchi	Bit like a hippo with a crew cut	#1
Masktchi	Like a sheep with a cat's head!	#1
Tarakotchi	Lippy thing with spindly legs	#1
Nyorotchi	Round lippy thing with long tail	#1
Mimitchi	Like a mametchi with larger pigtails	#2
Pochitchi	Like a big fluffy puppy	#2
Kusatchi	A dancing, big-lipped flower in a plantpot	#2
Takotchi	Octopus with a silly hat	#2
Hashizotchi	Big fat bird with stubby wings	#2
Zukitchi	Like a little devil	#2

Special

Oyajitchi	Head of bearded man with sticky up hair/spindly legs	#1*
Ketotchi	Man's head with beret (could be weird hair)	#1
Sekitoritchi	Big fat sumo wrestler	#2

Afterlife

Obaketchi	Wriggly soul and gravestone†
Angel-gotchi	Angel

* Only available in the Japanese version #1, replaced by ketotchi abroad
† Japan only.

COPING WITH VIRTUAL GRIEF

There's no avoiding it, your egglet will eventually leave you. Every egglet owner needs to know before they begin that one day they will find that their virtual pet has gone away. No matter how kind you are to your egglet, no matter how much time you spend looking after it, you must prepare yourself for the inevitable. It will die.

First, I'd better answer a very common question. People want to know how long they can expect their egglet to stay alive, and the answer is that it really depends on you. The current record is about 30 human days, although if you were ever lucky enough to rear a perfect (almost impossible) egglet, in theory it could last a couple of weeks longer than that.

LIFESPAN	BRONWEN SAYS:
0–5 days	Either you haven't read this book or you have your own version of my brother Ken, who has been sneaking into your room and torturing your egglet. Try again.

6–10 days	Well, it's better than nothing. I mean, at least you managed to keep your egglet alive until it became an adult. Still not amazing though, next time try playing with it more, and checking up on it more often.
11–16 days	You have the true mark of a tamagotchi parent. This is a very respectable lifespan for the average egglet. Try experimenting next time with a slightly different style, just in case you can make your next pet's lifespan last longer.
17–22 days	If you managed to keep a virtual pet alive for this long without reading this book, then I don't think you need to read this book at all. You're a natural. Excellent work.
23 days +	You're one in a million. Are you sure we're not related?

There is, in fact, a secret way of ageing your tamagotchi which my brother Ken discovered, but it caused so much trouble it hurts just to talk about it. None of his pets ever survived very long, but he came to me one day and told me that he'd heard about a trick that would make your egglet appear as old as you wanted.

All you have to do is call up the clock screen by pressing B. Then press A and C together to put it into SET mode. Using the A button, advance the clock forward twelve hours until the time is the same but the AM (or PM) has changed to PM (or AM). Press C to start the clock again, and your egglet should immediately beep for attention because it'll probably be bedtime.

Immediately call up the clock screen again and advance the hours another twelve hours so that the time is back where you started (in other words, the time is right again). Press C to activate the clock again and go and check your egglet's Health Monitor. With any luck, you should find that your pet is a whole year older. And you can repeat this little trick as often as you want, until your egglet is positively ancient.

OK, it all seems very simple, doesn't it? I don't know what came over me, but I tried it out on Migi. I went through the process in the way Ken had told me, and sure enough my little Migi was another tamagotchi year older when I finished. Well, I thought, that's interesting. Except when I woke up the next day, Migi was dead.

I hadn't thought Ken's scam through properly, and the only reason I'm telling you this is so you don't make the same mistake that I did. Yes, Migi aged a year in a matter of minutes, but think of what else happened inside his poor little head. In his accelerated, time travel world inside the casing, a whole human day had passed without any Meals, without any Snacks, and without any playtime. He must have thought I'd disappeared off the face of the Earth. What would have happened if he became ill during that period? Perhaps he did, because I had no way of knowing.

With 20/20 hindsight, there may have been a way to avoid such a disaster. For example, if I'd made sure that Migi was stuffed full of food and as happy as possible before I started, and then turned the light out before I moved the clock back round for the last twelve hours. But now it's too late, and Migi is gone for ever. And all for what? Just to make him a little bit older. I realize now what Ken was up to. He and his friends used to have egglet death races to see how fast they could kill theirs off. But clearly they've now realized that it's much cleverer to see who can keep their egglet alive the longest. But Ken being Ken, he was too dishonourable to actually try and treat his egglet properly. Instead, he devoted all his efforts to finding a shortcut, and it was a shortcut that proved fatal for poor Migi.

So, what happens when a tamagotchi dies? It'll start bleeping in a steady rhythm, like one of those heart monitors in a hospital. The worried egglet owner rushes to see what the problem is, but none of the buttons respond. It just keeps beeping, the beeps getting slower and slower, until it just plain stops. With certain egglets, you may see a brief flash as an egg appears on the screen. This could be the creature's little life flashing before its eyes, but I like to think it's a premonition of new life to come, as the dying egglet is permitted a vision of reincarnation ahead. Then you will see the smiling angel on the screen.

The only button that responds is the C button, which will tell you how old your egglet was when it passed away.

No matter how well you've looked after your egglet, the first feeling you get is guilt. Even though all pets will eventually die, a lot of owners will walk around blaming themselves. If only I'd played with it just a little bit more, they say. If only I didn't feed it so many Snacks. If only I'd cleaned up the poo faster. Maybe I disciplined it too much. Maybe I didn't discipline it enough. If only I'd turned the light off earlier that time.

But it's too late now, and you shouldn't blame yourself. As long as you did your best, you have nothing to feel sorry about. Your egglet's days are numbered from the moment it hatches, so it's important that you give it all the love and attention that you can while it's alive, not agonize about it after it's too late to make a difference. If your egglet has had a happy, carefree life with a kind owner, it couldn't possibly wish for more.

There are egglet graveyards on the Internet where you can register your pet's name and appearance, and get a little headstone in loving memory. If you can get on the Internet you can pop over to the gravesite and visit your egglet, but do remember that all you're looking at is a representation of it. Your real egglet isn't there, you're just looking at a virtual stone; your real egglet is somewhere else, flitting around having a whale of a time. Tamagotchi turn into angels in the same way that caterpillars turn into butterflies. Don't be sad that your virtual pet isn't with you any longer. Be happy that it has gone on to experience new things, and content that, for a brief time, you were able to share in its life.

Remember that when you are rearing a virtual pet it is the journey, not the destination, that is important. It doesn't matter once your egglet is dead whether or not you could have done things differently. What matters is that while your egglet was alive you were happy together, and shared each other's lives. No one can ever take away your happy memories, your chats with your friends about your egglet's little quirks, or perhaps the pictures that you drew of your pet's changing appearance. Nobody owns a tamagotchi. You might own the little plastic case with the screen in it, but the creature that grows up inside belongs to itself, and will eventually have to go off and get on with the next step.

But of course, if you still own the plastic case with the screen in it, there's absolutely nothing there to stop you hatching a new virtual pet, and trying again.

STARTING OVER

Your egglet angel will flit around your screen for as long as you want it to. It's probably a good idea not to rush off immediately and hatch a new one. Why not think for a while about things you could do differently the next time? You can also chat to your friends, because if they have their own egglet they will also have to deal with the same sort of problem.

← MATERNITY WARD

Some people swear that they will never again try and rear a virtual pet because they were so heartbroken when their first egglet died. If you feel that way, my advice is to leave it for a while and see how you feel in a few days. Because if you really cared that much about your first egglet, the chances are that you are a perfect candidate for the best egglet owner in the world. Someone like my brother Ken, who'll just say 'Oops! There goes another one,' and immediately hatch a replacement, is never going to be a good egglet owner. But someone who genuinely cares about their egglet, who misses their pet's little smiling face and playtimes, is the kind of person that a young egglet really needs!

Maybe you could have done better, but so what, you did your best and that's all that counts. If you don't get back out there and rear another egglet, then your next pet might find itself in the hands of Ken or someone even worse, and you wouldn't want that, would you? You might not be perfect, but you're the best there is and there's a tamagotchi out there waiting for you to love it and care for it. Don't let it down.

Once you feel ready to try again with a new egglet, wave goodbye to the angel of your previous pet and press the A and C buttons simultaneously. You may need to press the reset button at the back of the casing, in which case you will also need to reset the clock (see Hatching). You should then see a throbbing egg on the screen just like last time. This is your new egglet getting ready to be born. Be ready to welcome it with open arms.

BRONWEN'S TAMAGOTCHI EXAM

So, are you a tamagotchi expert or are you the world's worst virtual pet owner? I've written a little quiz here for you to test your tamagotchi aptitude. Each question has three possible answers, (a), (b) and (c). Some have only one correct answer, others have one very correct answer and another that's not quite as good but which still scores. Don't write in the book, because you might want to test your friends or come back later and try again for a higher score. Just write down your answers to each question on a separate piece of paper and then check the answers printed at the end. I'm warning you now, some of the questions on this test are really fiendish, so don't even think about trying it until you've read the whole book. Ready? Let's go.

Questions

1   **Tamagotchi originally come from**
   a)   Japan
   b)   Somewhere very far away
   c)   Italy

2   **The word 'tamagotchi' means**
   a)   'Watch tower Mine shaft'
   b)   'Lovable Egg' or 'Egg Watch'
   c)   'Virtual Pet'

3 **The bat and ball icon means**
a) Play Game
b) Punish
c) Swim

4 **When you activate your tamagotchi the first thing you should do is**
a) Go on holiday
b) Set the clock
c) Feed it

5 **If the Hungry Monitor shows four white hearts, your tamagotchi is**
a) Full
b) Empty
c) In love

6 **Your tamagotchi's favourite food is**
a) Meals
b) Raw fish
c) Snacks

7 **The healthiest thing for your tamagotchi to eat is**
a) Meals
b) Raw fish
c) Snacks

8 **If your tamagotchi eats a Meal it will be**
a) Less hungry
b) 1oz heavier and one heart fuller
c) 2oz heavier and one heart happier

9 **Each Snack your tamagotchi eats makes it**
   a) Less hungry
   b) 1oz heavier and one heart fuller
   c) 2oz heavier and one heart happier

10 **If your tamagotchi is unhappy, the best way to cheer it up is**
   a) Play a game
   b) Give it a Snack
   c) Give it a Meal

11 **If your tamagotchi refuses to eat a Meal you should**
   a) Smack it
   b) Check the Health Monitor to make sure it's not already full
   c) Bribe it with a Snack

12 **Playing a game with a tamagotchi doesn't just cheer it up. It also**
   a) Makes it lose weight
   b) Makes it hungrier
   c) Helps cure a tamagotchi illness

13 **If your tamagotchi does a poo on the floor you should**
   a) Smack it, then clean it up
   b) Clean it up, then smack it
   c) Clean it up

14 **When your tamagotchi goes to sleep you should**
   a) Wake it up to make sure it's all right
   b) Turn the light out
   c) Just leave it alone

15 **If your tamagotchi is still ill after an injection you should**
   a) Give up and press the reset button
   b) Give it more injections until its better
   c) Give it a Snack and hope it gets better on its own

16 A healthy tamagotchi should grow at roughly

a) 1oz per day until it reaches 10oz

b) 10oz per day until it reaches 99oz

c) 10oz per day until it reaches 999oz

17 The average tamagotchi lives for about

a) Two weeks

b) Four weeks

c) Four months

18 To keep a tamagotchi quiet you can

a) Unscrew the back and rip out the speaker

b) Discipline it three times in a row and then press C

c) Press C and A to initiate the stealth mode

19 A baby tamagotchi will grow into the next stage in the life cycle

a) After 60 minutes

b) After 60 minutes unless bedtime comes first

c) After two hours

20 A child tamagotchi (series #1) is called a 'marutchi' because

a) It just is

b) It's Japanese for 'child'

c) It's Japanese for 'roundy-thing'

21 The oyajitichi special character is very hard to get on a non-Japanese tamagotchi because

a) It only exists on Japanese tamagotchi

b) It takes a lot of effort and luck to rear the special character

c) You need to keep it completely happy at all times for a whole two weeks

22 **Tamagotchi were the brainchild of a lady called**

a)   Yoko Ono
b)   Usagi Tsukino
c)   Aki Maita

23 **Developing the tamagotchi took**
a)   A total of three years
b)   A total of five years
c)   A total of ten years

24 **The digital monster (series #3) is different from other tamagotchi because**
a)   It has a gold-plated casing and a special clip to hang it on your belt
b)   It has a rectangular casing and a strong key chain
c)   It bounces when you drop it

25 **The Cleaning icon is a little duck because**
a)   It's a picture of Muramasa, the famous toilet-cleaning duck of Japanese legend
b)   When you press the icon, a little duck come in and cleans up the poo
c)   Some children's potties are made in the shape of a duck

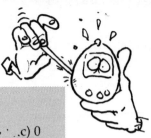

Answers

1	a) 2	b) 1	c) 0
2	a) 0	b) 2	c) 0
3	a) 2	b) 0	c) 0
4	a) 0	b) 2	c) 0
5	a) 0	b) 2	c) 0
6	a) 0	b) 0	c) 2
7	a) 2	b) 0	c) 0
8	a) 1	b) 2	c) 0
9	a) 0	b) 0	c) 2
10	a) 2	b) 1	c) 0
11	a) 0	b) 2	c) 0
12	a) 2	b) 0	c) 0
13	a) 0	b) 0	c) 2
14	a) 0	b) 2	c) 0
15	a) 0	b) 2	c) 0
16	a) 0	b) 2	c) 0
17	a) 2	b) 0	c) 0
18	a) 0	b) 0	c) 2
19	a) 1	b) 2	c) 0
20	a) 1	b) 0	c) 2
21	a) 2	b) 1	c) 0
22	a) 0	b) 0	c) 2
23	a) 2	b) 0	c) 0
24	a) 0	b) 2	c) 0
25	a) 0	b) 2	c) 0

How Did You Do?

If You Scored 1-10 Points

Hello Ken, I didn't know you were reading this book. But I don't think you've paid very close attention at all. You don't even know the basics! A most dishonourable score.

If You Scored 11-24 Points

Below average. You're still a couple of chopsticks short of a banquet. You know a few things about tamagotchi, but most of it is still a bit of a mystery to you. Try harder next time.

If You Scored 25 Points

Average. There are several areas of tamagotchi care that you're a little unclear on. Reread the relevant chapters and give it another go.

If You Scored 26-39 Points

Very good. You seem to know plenty about tamagotchi. There's just a couple of areas that you don't know by heart yet, so see if you can try a bit harder on them. Can you work out what they are? A very honourable score.

If You Scored 40-49 Points

Excellent. You have the makings of a truly successful tamagotchi owner. Don't worry if you made a couple of mistakes, because I deliberately put some questions in the exam that were almost impossible for anyone except a tamagotchi expert.

If You Scored 50 Points

Perfect. Congratulations, you are definitely a tamagotchi expert. You are probably my long-lost cousin or something like that. Your tamagotchi is happy and well, and you are a very nice and honourable person.

If You Scored More Than 50 Points

Er ... Ken? You can't get more than 50 points on this test. Stop cheating.

Thank you for reading my book. I hope that you and your tamagotchi are very happy together. We don't like to say goodbye in Japan. Instead we say 'see you again.' So if you want to see me again, you can find me where we first met, back in the first chapter. See you there.

Love, Bronwen